"A Woman for All Seasons is an outstanding example of how Mary's journey of faith can deepen our own relationship to God and others throughout the seasons of our lives. It is my hope it will contribute to authentic devotion to Mary."

Rev. Msgr. Sam R. Miglarese, V.G.
Diocese of Charleston

"Sally Moran—wife, mother, career woman—reflects on the seasons of a woman's life. Using the Scriptural stories of Mary and readings for the liturgical year as starting points, she throws the warm light of her wisdom and experience on the whole range of women's experience. Career, marriage, pregnancy, child-rearing, family life, widowhood, the single state—Sally Moran finds guidance and support in all of these through her conversation with the biblical and liturgical tradition.

"While she writes for women, men will profit from her book not only in being guided by a thoughtful woman in reflection on women's experiences, but also in adapting to their own lives her spiritual insights."

Emil A. Wcela
Auxiliary Bishop
Diocese of Rockville Centre

"A Woman for All Seasons is a book not only to help you ponder, as Mary did, but also to be affirmed and called to be fully present to your own life experiences, as Mary was. I especially appreciate Mary, the *woman*, as companion, welcoming me into autumn and walking with me into winter. Sally Moran has pondered long on Mary, Scripture, the Liturgical Year, and life. What a gift to us is this integration!"

Rose T. Vermette, R.C.D.
Spiritual Director
Archdiocese of New York

D0061862

"The scenes of Mary's lifetime, the vivid and forceful descriptions of the seasons and the skill with which the author weaves the golden threads of Mary's existence among the more ordinary fibers of everyday life are of equal excellence in this literary work. *A Woman for All Seasons* succeeds in assisting the reader to replace the 'sanctimonious, mythical' Mary with the Semitic peasant maiden with roughened hands and sun-darkened skin. This maiden knew a life not too unlike that of the out of wedlock teenager, or the woman in her 'summer years' who is 'caught up in competition, ambition, self-fulfillment.' This very similarity can strengthen and guide women today in finding the Christian and sometimes even simply the ethical answer to the questions and challenges that beseige them in today's world."

Joan Daria, R.N., Ed.D.
New Lisbon, N.J. Development Center

SALLY MORAN

REFLECTIONS ON MARY

TWENTY-THIRD PUBLICATIONS
Mystic, Connecticut 06355

To John
Companion throughout all the seasons

Illustrations by William Baker

Twenty-Third Publications
185 Willow Street
P.O. Box 180
Mystic CT 06355
(203) 536-2611
800-321-0411

ISBN 0-89622-531-3
Library of Congress Catalog Card Number 92-60892

PREFACE

Several years ago I determined to write this book. My life seemed agreeable enough: a loving, successful husband, three adult children settled into their careers and families, a comfortable home in a lovely community, and two much loved elderly cats. My career provided me with satisfaction and a respectable degree of success. In gratitude, I thought, I should write this book to honor Mary of Nazareth, the Mother of Christ.

The book would be arranged according to seasons, the naturally occurring seasons of the year compared with the chronological seasons of women's lives. The feasts of the liturgical seasons would be reviewed to offer insight and guidance as we journeyed through the seasons of our lives. Mary would be our role model, because, like us, she grew from her youth/spring to her old age/winter.

Since I was fairly well educated, had been published before, and regarded myself as a mature Catholic Christian, I felt confident I could write this book.

That was several years ago.

In the meantime, a tragic event profoundly affected me. Someone very dear to me told me that she has an incurable disease. All through my life I had prayed faithfully to Mary, but now I felt Mary had broken faith with me. For months, stunned with grief and crippled with anger, I raged at God and Mary. Eventually my impoverished soul spent its fury. Grief is manageable now, only sporadically breaking through.

And, of course, Mary is still present. I realize now that Mary knows my—our—suffering. She can identify with us. She knew homelessness, exile, poverty. She experienced apparently illegitimate pregnancy, and widowhood. She was in Jerusalem and heard the mob screaming for her son's life. She felt fury, fear, and prejudice when she was at Calvary. She listened to her son's moans and watched the life leak out of him. She witnessed his death and held him against her heart. Mary saw his ashen body placed in the dark tomb. Yes, Mary understands the human condition.

Today, as the winter of my life grows deeper, and I feel far less confident, I humbly present this book to honor Mary of Nazareth, the Mother of Christ.

CONTENTS

INTRODUCTION

Throughout the world, woman is found in every walk of life from chattel to head of state. She may be respected and fulfilled, or abused and dejected.

Where is her role model, her advocate? One might propose Mary of Nazareth, but not the Mary who has evolved into a plaster-of-paris statue, demure, sanctimonious, mythical. To appreciate Mary, we must strip her of the accumulation of centuries of romantic pietistic lore. Set aside for the moment the blond, blue-eyed woman classically draped and crowned with stars. Forget the silent statue gazing down at votive candles flickering in an empty church. Remember that Mary is a historical figure, a woman who existed in a specific place and time. What was the world like when Mary lived? Not too different from current times when one looks at the political and social issues of her day.

Cleopatra had recently committed suicide in Egypt. Julius Caesar and Pompey had been assassinated. Caesar Augustus had succeeded to the throne in Rome. The Roman Empire extended eastward to Persia (currently Iran), westward to Spain, southward to Africa, and northward to Germany. The emperor was beginning to look toward the conquest of Britain. King Herod the Great, a ruthless quisling, sat on the throne at Jerusalem.

The Jewish people resentfully submitted to the hateful occupation by Roman legions. Amid seditious plots, they anxiously waited for a military Messiah who would overthrow Rome and restore Israel to free nationhood. Mary lived within this political tension.

Scripture is economical in dealing with Mary. Little is given to us, but one fact is there for all to discover: Mary, like each of us, grew and developed in her journey through her allotted time. From her first question, "But how shall this be done?" to her last directive, "Do whatever he tells you," one can trace the maturation of her soul.

SPRING

"Come, then, my love...
For see, winter is past,
the rains are over and gone...."
Song of Songs 2:10-11

Spring is the season that extends from the vernal equinox to the summer solstice, the time when this spinning old planet once again tilts toward the sun-star. The sun climbs higher, and days lengthen. Caribou, deer, and elk cross the northern tundra. Birds no larger than one's fist ride the sky with majestic geese, swans, and loons as they migrate north.

Tiny rodents and huge lumbering bear emerge from hibernation. As the soil warms, bulbs push upward. Crocus, hyacinth, tulips, and daffodils sparkle in the sunlight. In the great mountains, streams flow seaward once again. Wildflowers cover the hillsides and prairies with shimmering color. Bees and butterflies pollinate the flowers, adding their own loveliness to the surroundings. Farmers plow and plant, confident that once again Earth will receive the seed and provide crops.

For many of us who live in urban or suburban areas, this annual phenomenon is largely missed. We encounter spring in a more subtle way. Bunches of pussywillows or forsythia appear in florist shops and next to wooden fences. The homeless sleep in the park now instead of in doorways. Tax time comes again. Soccer balls and skateboards reappear. School proms, final exams, and baseball's spring training become priority considerations. Windows need washing; closets are rearranged. The pace of life quickens. A hint of joy stirs within many of us.

Spring is a season of promise, renewal, regrowth. It is usually portrayed with symbols of early life: bunnies, cherubs, chicks. A person in the springtime of life is perceived to be energetic, full of promise. Youth is the springtime of one's life.

YOUTHFUL MARY

*"Many women have done admirable things,
but you surpass them all."*

Proverbs 31:29

Mary was a Semitic peasant maiden, most likely dark-haired, swarthy, clad in rough, hand-woven garments. She was intimate with sheep raising, wool gathering, and weaving. Her tasks included collecting the scarce well water, baking bread, raising herbs and vegetables, helping with the laborious work of laundering, child care, tending the sick and aged. Most probably her hands were rough, her skin sun-darkened. Mary endured the oppressive heat of the day and shivered in the cold nights. She accompanied her parents annually to Jerusalem for festivals, when she danced and sang, played and prayed. She was bound by tribal customs and a body of religious law that dictated strict adherence to prayer, behavior, and diet codes.

Mary was no more than fourteen or fifteen when she was betrothed to Joseph. There was no dating, no falling in love. Most likely, her future husband was selected by her father, since in her culture betrothal was a formal state based upon mutual contract between families. The couple was considered married in every sense except physical union.

CHOICES

"I will be with you as I was with Moses;
I will not leave you or desert you."

Joshua 1:5

Psychiatry, society, and culture have assigned specific developmental tasks to every age of humankind. The tasks of youth include pivotal choices about one's selfhood, philosophy, behavior, and career.

In the springtime of her life, Mary, like us, was faced with choices. At some point during her betrothal Mary was faced with an astounding situation, a monumental choice. Luke (1:26-28), in the spare language of Scripture, tells us that "the angel Gabriel was sent by God." Luke describes Mary as "greatly troubled." Her initial reaction was fear. How very much like us. We live with fear. There is global fear—of nuclear war, crime, disease—and there is individual fear. Children fear the dark, school; ad-

olescents fear isolation, rejection; adults fear failure, poverty. We all fear loneliness and death. And yet, how often the Scriptures say, "Fear not" or "Do not be afraid."

Zechariah was told, "Do not be afraid...your prayer is heard." Joseph was told, "Do not fear to take Mary as your wife." The shepherds were told, "Be not afraid." Yet everyone walks with fear. How did Mary respond to her fear? Mary questioned the angel, "How can this be, since I have no husband?"

The angel spoke to her. Mary listened and then made her magnificent choice: "Let it be done to me according to your word."

The twentieth century is the century of communication. Millions of dollars are spent annually on books, essays, videotapes, seminars devoted to the development of communication, problem-solving and decision-making skills. Managers are expected to listen, gather relevant data, formulate sound decisions. The upwardly mobile liberated female must master communication skills. Well educated, astute, assertive, she is expected to listen, question, decide.

Would anyone expect a peasant maiden of two thousand years ago to relate to the modern career woman? Could she have any relevant skill? Yet, Mary questioned the angel. She listened, then made her decision. Nineteen centuries before the advent of multi-media presentations, Mary had mastered those skills that are still considered fundamental today. Is it not appropriate for the young career woman of today to look to Mary of Nazareth for help and guidance?

LIBERATION

"You were called, as you know, to liberty;
but be careful, or this liberty will provide an opening
for self-indulgence."

Galatians 5:13

In the springtime of life Mary listened, decided, acted. Her choice liberated all of us. But like most of us, her liberation did not simplify her life. In fact, her "yes" complicated it.

We are told that Mary went "to the hill country of Judea" to be with Elizabeth (Luke 1:39). Did she make this long journey perhaps to share her momentous news with Elizabeth? To seek affirmation of her experience?

In those days it was no small feat for a female to undertake a three-day journey. Most likely the Roman army of occupation discouraged travel by the local people. Mary's trip involved travel along the main road to Jerusalem. She would encounter caravans from afar as well as local travelers. There were Roman soldiers in the area,

posing the timeless threat to females: drunkenness, robbery, rape. There were the usual thieves plying their trade. Furthermore, custom forbade a woman to travel unaccompanied. A companion or two would have been sought to make the journey with her. Much of the trip would be on foot except for short respites on a donkey. Despite the discouragement and danger implicit in all these factors, Mary set out for Elizabeth's village.

Today, despite technological innovations, isn't travel fraught with danger? Do we not hear of kidnapping, bomb threats, hijacking, mugging, rape, not to mention the common inconveniences of car and plane travel?

The liberation of female culture has indeed complicated the lives of young women. Traditional roles have been challenged. Decisions must be made on every level: intra-familial, inter-personal, vocational, educational. Formulating one's philosophical and spiritual commitment is a challenging, often painful experience. Here we can see again the threads of similarity woven through the life of Mary of Nazareth and our lives as modern women.

HASTE

"You worry and fret about so many things."

Luke 10:41

Mary set out for Elizabeth's village. She went in haste.
Haste...what does the young woman of the twentieth century know of haste? The American lifestyle is full of haste.
By the time a young female is in high school she has become imbued with a sense of haste. Her day is packed
with school time, extracurricular activities, an after-school
job, telephone, television, social time. There aren't
enough hours in a given day to accomplish all the required tasks. She is hassled, frazzled, hustled.

When the young woman goes on to college or to the
world of work, nothing changes very much. She is still frenetically busy. Activities are substituted, not eliminated.
She also jogs or bicycles, plays racquetball or tennis. Frequently her day begins with a quick gulp of coffee or juice
and some twelve to sixteen hours
later, she crumples into exhausted
sleep. Indeed, she has hastened to
her own particular hill country.

But let us pause a moment.
Mary hastened to Elizabeth.
Then what? Luke (1:39-56) describes the event: "She went
into Zechariah's house and
greeted Elizabeth." After the

noise and dirt of the uncomfortable trip she "went in...and greeted Elizabeth." Mary stepped inside, away from the oppressive, sun-blanched heat to the cool quiet of her cousin's home. She "greeted Elizabeth."

Here was a young maiden in the springtime of her life traveling for days to greet an old woman who was in the winter of her years. Mary, steeped in her culture, respectfully offered a salutation of respect and love. But Elizabeth "in a loud voice cries out." This was an interesting reversal. Elderly Elizabeth, like a roaring spring stream unable to be contained by its banks, bursts forth, "...the moment your greeting reached my ears, the child in my womb leapt for joy."

Already Mary's ministry has begun. She was God's herald, bringing joy and freedom. She gave her decision, her yes to God. She burdened herself by traveling to Elizabeth, who recognized her as "the mother of my Lord." Mary brought joy to the unborn child, John, whose sensitive soul stirred in recognition of his God, nestled within Mary's virginal womb.

Mary's haste had a specific goal. Her hill country was an actual place. Too often, in our haste, we feel we are caught, spinning our wheels. We too must "go in and greet" our God. Take time out. Fifteen minutes early in the day or during lunch break or before bed. Give up a few minutes of sleep, exercise, conversation, or television. These few minutes, this precious time, will help you to be like Mary.

MAGNIFICAT

"Bless Yahweh, my soul."

Psalm 103:1

Mary, "who believed that the promise made her by the Lord would be fulfilled" (Luke 1:38), delivered her Magnificat. She demonstrated through her hymn of praise an impressive knowledge of Scripture coupled with keen political awareness. Her choice of words linked her with Hannah, the mother of Samuel, and with Miriam, the sister of Moses.

Again, as with Elizabeth, a juxtaposition existed between youth and age. Hannah was married many years and appeared to be barren. Only after years of continuous, tearful supplication to Yahweh did Hannah conceive and bear a son, the prophet and judge Samuel. Conversely, Miriam began her work as a young girl when she guarded her brother Moses as he lay hidden among reeds (Exodus 2:4-7). When the Pharaoh's daughter found Moses, Miriam had shrewdly arranged for his own mother to act as his governess in the Egyptian palace.

Aged Hannah, barren, delivered a son, Samuel, who anointed Saul, the first king of Israel. Aged Elizabeth, barren, carried John, who baptized Jesus, the Messiah.

Miriam, a young girl, provided for Moses' safety, thereby allowing him to deliver the Israelites to the Promised Land. Mary, a young girl, provided Jesus with his humanity, thereby allowing him to deliver humankind to redemption.

Upon dedicating her son to Yahweh, Hannah delivered her canticle of praise (Samuel 2:1-11), foreshadowing Mary's Magnificat. Miriam, upon the safe crossing of the Sea of Reeds, picked up her timbrel and led the Israelites in their joyous anthem (Exodus 15:1-21).

In her Magnificat, Mary's soul reflects her joy in God. In it she expresses her own role in history and acknowledges the fulfillment of the promise of the Messiah. In it she speaks out to women for all seasons.

HOME

"For the sons of the forsaken one are more in number than the sons of the wedded wife," says Yahweh.

Isaiah 54:1

According to Luke, Mary remained with Elizabeth for about three months and then went back home. Back home...what images the words convey! There is the Victorian version of a well-furnished home with smiling children, loving mother, and beneficent father; the happy television family where the father always wears a tie; the crowded vermin-infested quarters of the ghetto; the cardboard box of the homeless; the one-parent abode of the divorced, widowed, or unmarried mother. All too often, home is not where the heart is. Home can mean estrangement, isolation, abuse, instead of the cradle of love where one's outlook on life is formed.

Mary returned home from Elizabeth's. Matthew (1:18-25) describes succinctly how Mary, some time later, before she and Joseph "came to live together...was found to be with child through the Holy Spirit." Jewish law was very explicit concerning unwed pregnancy. A betrothed virgin who was with child "must be taken out to the gate of the town" and stoned to death (Deuteronomy 22:23-24). In electing to put her away privately, Joseph had saved Mary's life. But why was there such lack of communication? Was Mary's pregnancy unknown until she returned home? Had Joseph noticed a subtle change in Mary's silhouette? Had Mary explained about the visit from Gabriel? Either Mary explained what happened and Joseph did not believe her, or she remained silent. Why would Mary have refrained from sharing her knowledge of the Messiah with Joseph, particularly after the events that took place at Elizabeth and Zechariah's home? Speculation about this circumstance yields little except the realization that both Mary and Joseph spent hours agonizing separately. Each suffered, and each suffered alone.

Where were Mary's parents during this time? Scripture does not mention them. Did they also wonder about her pregnancy? Was Mary estranged from them?

Like countless young women today, Mary knew the fear of an illegitimate pregnancy. She knew shame, loneliness, rejection. She actually feared for her life: stoning according to the law. Like countless members of her sex, Mary must have shed bitter tears over her situation. Not until the intervention of an angel did Joseph relent and take "his wife to his home."

FEELINGS

"Enough for me to keep my soul tranquil."

Psalm 131:2

When Joseph finally accepted Mary, how did she feel? Was she resentful of Joseph's attitude? Did she feel abandoned by God? Perhaps she doubted the reality of her interaction with Gabriel. When she performed the mundane tasks of wifehood, was she contented? How was the mother of the "son of the most high" just another pregnant wife in the village of Nazareth? These answers are not found in Scripture.

For us women today, we should find some consolation in that fact. Like Mary, we are beset with problems for which there seem to be no clear answers. Are we better than Mary? Since Mary had to struggle in faith through situations similar to ours, we can expect her understanding and intercession. We can appeal to her for help and comfort. Like Mary, we believe that the promise "made by the Lord" will be fulfilled.

Like the tide of women through history, Mary washed, mended, cleaned, cooked. She mingled with other women, prayed, and waited. Her body swelled with her growing child. She was tired and ungainly. Throughout the hot summer she waited, all the while performing the repetitive, boring tasks of being a wife and expectant mother.

Remember, then, that Mary was real, all human. When loneliness, fatigue, misunderstanding, and disappointment weary your spirit, Mary knew—knows—such feelings. She persevered to the end, believing "that the promise made her by the Lord would be fulfilled" (Luke 1:38). In our own dark moments, we too must persevere. Remember that we—each of us—are part of the Lord's promise.

MARY TODAY

"All generations will call me blessed."

Luke 1:48

If we were to encounter Mary today, what would she be like? As she was in Nazareth, so she would be today: a young female of her culture, her historical era. She would be influenced by her family's customs and follow a body of religious law. At fifteen or sixteen, she would be attending school, would look unremarkable, have her favorite music group, enjoy sports, singing, and dancing. She would probably have an after-school job, and, like so many adolescents, would volunteer time for her favorite causes: helping the aged, raising money for the hungry, tutoring an underprivileged child, participating in youth ministry.

Mary made her choice and assented to God twenty centuries ago. If she existed in our culture today, she would meet its challenges and would still give her "yes" to her creator. Remember her Magnificat. It revealed a knowledge of Scripture, related its author to two important women of history, and acknowledged the beginning of the Messianic Age. Would Mary be less astute, less courageous, less committed to her outlook today?

MISSION

"Do whatever he tells you."

John 2:6

Like Mary, each one of us has a spiritual mission, a task specific to one's time, one's place, one's existence. Like her, each of us has a choice to make. Like hers, our youthful choices will influence our lives and the lives of others. Our choices must always reflect decisions based upon the deep awareness that we are special to God.

We too, in the springtime of our lives, must be aware of our specific spiritual mission, and give our unconditional "yes" to God.

ANNUNCIATION
"Holy is his name."

Luke 1:49

Spring's liturgical calendar is rich with spiritual signifi-
cance. The readings from the Mass for the Annunciation,
March 25, refer to a prophecy dating from around 800
B.C.: "The virgin shall be with child, and bear a son, and
shall name him Immanuel" (Isaiah 7:10-14). As Matthew
tells us (1:23-24), Immanuel means "God is with us."
What comfort for us. Early in the springtime of the year
we are reminded of God's abiding presence. The responsorial psalm from the day's Mass is "Here I am, Lord; I
come to do your will." What a simple but gargantuan
task: "to do your will." Yet if we remember Mary, the adolescent who was "deeply troubled," we can take
strength from that thought, make our fundamental
choice, and give our "yes" to God, confident that God is,
indeed, with us.

LENT

"Do not provoke the anger of the Lord."

Judith 8:14

Consistent with the tumultuous tension of adolescence and young adulthood is the season of Lent. On Ash Wednesday, Jesus instructs us how to perform good deeds, fast, and pray (Matthew 6:1-6,16-18). On Thursday after Ash Wednesday Jesus exhorts us, "Take up the cross every day and follow me" (Luke 9:23-24). The liturgy for Friday after Ash Wednesday explains the lifestyle God wants for us: "Share your bread with the hungry, shelter the homeless poor, clothe the person you see to be naked, and do not turn from your kin" (Isaiah 58:7-8).

The liturgy of Lent is replete with trials and tribulations. God sent the deluge to cover Earth, sparing only Noah and the inhabitants of the Ark (Genesis 9:8-15, Year B of the Liturgical Calendar). We are told that Noah "alone" of all the people listened to God's call. To stand alone is particularly difficult in adolescence. The springtime of life is when we seek affirmation from our peers; we yearn to be part of the group. Yet Noah alone listened to God's call. That call is often obscured in the noisy, busy days of our lives.

Abraham was asked to sacrifice his only son, Isaac (Genesis 22:1-2,9-13,15-18). Abraham had remained childless to old age, yet, despite the passing of years before

God's promise was fulfilled, Abraham held true to his faith. That faith must have been sorely tested. He and Sarah had aged, but God had promised him that his descendants would be as numerous as the sands of the seashore. Eventually, his wife gave birth to Isaac. Then God—illogically, we would think—asked Abraham to sacrifice his beloved son. With his unconditional "yes" to God, Abraham foreshadowed Mary.

Adolescence is the time when one's faith-philosophy is honed. One is moving from the rather simplistic outlook of childhood toward the complexity of adulthood. The adolescent seeks ideals and role models. Heroes must be strong, fair-minded, attractive, and, above all, successful; nobody wants to follow someone who isn't. And then we have Jesus: "The Son of Man came not to be served, but to serve, and to give his life as a ransom for many" (Matthew 20:28, Communion Antiphon, Wednesday, 2nd Week of Lent). What a contradiction! But what a challenge!

The lenten liturgies continue with the story of Jesus. The Transfiguration (gospel, 2nd Sunday of Lent) describes the brilliance of Jesus as he spoke with Moses the lawgiver and Elijah the prophet. God the Father tells them that Jesus is his Son and admonishes us to "listen to him."

In the gospel of the 3rd Sunday of Lent (Year B) the Jews demand signs (John 2:13-25) and the Greeks wisdom (1 Corinthians 1:22-25). Jesus expresses dismay at the commercial activity distracting from the sense of prayer within the Temple precincts so he expels the merchants from the place.

In the gospel for the 3rd Sunday of Lent (John 4:5-42, Year A) Jesus shocks his disciples by associating with the Samaritan woman. Not only was she considered an outcast by birth (Samaritan), but she was a behavioral outcast as well. Jesus consistently demonstrated great kindness and mercy for women who were ostracized. Perhaps in his youth, Mary told him of her fears before Joseph took her into his house. Was Jesus responding to his human feelings toward Mary as well as his divine mercy and love?

The parable of the Prodigal Son, in the gospel for the 4th Sunday of Lent (Luke 15:11-32, Year C), demonstrates God's consistent love for us, even when we foolishly squander our gifts. Like the Samaritan woman, we must tell others the truth about Jesus and, like the Prodigal Son, we must return to our Father. On the 4th Sunday of Lent (Year B) Jesus tells Nicodemus that the "Son of Man must be lifted up," referring to his death on the cross. Lent culminates in the death and resurrection of Jesus.

PASSION, DEATH, AND RESURRECTION OF JESUS

"As for me, give me courage."

Esther 4:17

Because we have viewed the crucifix all of our lives, we have become inured to the sight. Let us not forget that crucifixion is an ugly, slow, barbarously painful way to die. Legislators today who are in favor of the death penalty would never consider such a penalty for the most violent, sadistic, murderous felon. Yet Christ suffered such a death. And Mary was there. Her grief and horror were very real. The artistically beautiful Pieta doesn't come near portraying Mary's grief. Like so many mothers today, she lost her child.

Twentieth-century youth are dying in unprecedented numbers. Drugs and alcohol are slaughtering thousands on our highways, in school corridors, in the streets of our cities. Countless young are dying by their own hands: suicides.

Mothers lie awake at night, waiting for the return of their young adult or adolescent children. All too often, the dreaded phone call summons them to emergency rooms, jails, or even morgues. In that awful moment, Mary is present. She held her dead child in her arms; she felt the cold skin and saw the pallor of death. She watched him laid in the tomb. Mary had no marvelous intuition that the resurrection was imminent. She grieved, her heart broken with sorrow. Where was Mary's Magnificat on that dreadful day of loss?

When you are sick with grief, half-mad with despair, living your own Good Friday, remember Easter. On Easter morning, the women went to the tomb "while it was still dark." When it is still dark in your own life, remember the words of the angel at the tomb: "There is no need for you to be afraid." Fear cripples you, drains your reserve, clouds your judgment, feeds despair. In dark times, cling to the consciousness of Mary's existence.

EASTER...PENTECOST

"Rejoice heart and soul, daughter of Zion."

Zechariah 9:9

The joy of Easter, the glory of the resurrection, is so often lost to us. Yearly repetition of the feast (too often considered only a "holiday") dulls the reality of the event. We must take hold of the message of Easter: "I have risen; I am with you."

It is appropriate that Easter occurs in the spring, because it is the season of promise, of renewal. The youthful members of society are energetic, richly idealistic, ready to reform the world. All of us, energized by the reality of Easter, can renew ourselves, strengthen our resolve, face and overcome obstacles.

Following the promise of Easter are the feasts of the Ascension and Pentecost. These liturgical feasts are mirrors of human life: sorrow frequently preceding joy. The liturgical joy of Easter is preceded by the austere lenten study of the passion of Jesus. So, too, the separation of Jesus from the apostles, which took place at the Ascension, precedes Pentecost. The Acts of the Apostles tells us that "while they looked on...a cloud took [Jesus] from their sight."

Matthew writes that "the eleven" set out to meet Jesus before the Ascension; we can infer from Mark and Luke too that only the eleven were present at the Ascension. Mary was not present for this leave-taking. We are told, though, that prior to this she was present in the upper room, "joined in continuous prayer" (Acts 1:14). She must have been present at Pentecost, for "they had all met in one room."

Although this feast occurs in the springtime of the year, Mary's Pentecost occurred in the autumn or winter of her life. Her youthful "yes" found fulfillment in her later years. It is the same with us. The decisions of our youth will profoundly influence our lives...our summers, autumns, and winters. Be careful, then, of the decisions made in youth; they will affect your life.

Be mindful of Mary. She lived in an era of assassinations, poverty, political intrigue, military occupation, disease, and other social ills (not unlike our own times), but she did not reject the religious laws and customs of her parents. She used her intelligence to make decisions, and once she had made her commitment, she remained faithful to the end. Mary was a peasant maiden. But she also was—is—Messiah-mother, prophet, leader, herald, total woman, role model...role model for the women of this century in their youth, their springtime.

SUMMER

*"The pastures on the heath are green again,
the trees bear fruit,
vine and fig tree yield abundantly."*

Joel 2:22

Summer, extending from the summer solstice to the autumnal equinox, is the season when we witness delicate spring flowers yielding to voluptuous roses, colorful zinnias, stately columbine; fruit trees shedding their blossoms and bearing nourishing fruit. Trees are in full leaf, providing needed shade. The raucous songs of cicadas ring out along the roadside, and the chattering of redwing blackbirds rises from the meadow. Animals feed their young and teach them the skills they need for survival. Bees alight on flowers to gather nectar, and the air is filled with birdsong.

City streets are hot and hazy, and people seek relief in the park or under the sprinkler by the fire hydrant. Others picnic, barbecue, swim, sail, or set off for an extended vacation. With school recessed, children fill their time in carefree diversion. Graduations and weddings are common.

Women in the summer of their lives are deeply engaged in the process of living. They have embarked on courses set by their earlier choices. They may be involved in their careers, or working in relationships that ripened from courtship into marriage, perhaps bearing and rearing children, or living as a single person. They may be rearing children alone, having suffered the stunning pain of divorce or widowhood. Many are juggling the simultaneous demands of motherhood, wifehood, and career.

Like the season, women in their summer years are productive. Maturing from youthful exuberance, they provide the fabric that binds society together. Whether as homemakers, in the work force, or in the professions, women provide a consistent presence. They are nurturers, healers, innovators, leaders, entertainers, laborers, teachers, cleaners, dressmakers, counselors, life-bearers. Their tasks are countless, responsibilities awesome, and contributions honorable. Yet, much of what is provided by women is unsung. Like Mary in her summer years, their summer years are largely private.

EXILE

"Let him test me in the crucible.
I shall come out pure gold."

Job 23:10

In the summertime of her life, where was Mary? Like many women, she married, and like so many in today's mobile society, she traveled: to Bethlehem in response to Caesar's summons, to Egypt to flee Herod's threat, and back to Palestine. It was not an auspicious beginning for married life. Mary had prepared her home in Nazareth for the expected child. Perhaps she had asked Joseph to make a cradle for the child. Had she asked for any toys? Had she woven small garments? Most likely, few if any of their possessions were carried to Bethlehem. Later, the hasty departure by night for Egypt! And we think we are the only ones who have to rush from one place to the next.

Mary must have been lonely in Egypt, missing the village neighbors and the conversations with her kinswomen. There were no grandparents to enjoy her son. As immigrants in Egypt, they lived in a ghetto there, separated from the mainstream of society, marginalized as so many people are today. Like many women in our day, Mary was unable to provide what she had wished for her son. The quiet hours of planning and dreaming during her pregnancy did not include exile to an alien land. Like many working mothers or single parents, her plans for her son's childhood were substantially changed by uncontrollable events.

If you are concerned when you leave your child in day-care, or feel guilt because you must go to work when your child is ill, remember Mary. Like you, her early mothering was not always the way she had wanted it to be. She understands your circumstances and feelings better than you know. Direct your pain to Mary, who can provide you with guidance and strength.

RETURN

"And I called my son out of Egypt."

Matthew (2:20-21) tells us that Joseph took the child and his mother back to Galilee. Back again after years away, it was for Mary and Joseph a return home. For the young child Jesus, it was dislocation, loss of playmates, a different environment. Even here Mary is like us. Throughout history, prior to the Industrial Revolution, most people were born, lived, and died within the same locale. Yet Mary relocated several times within a few years before the family settled in Nazareth. How similar this is to the relocation that women do today!

In Luke, we are told that the Holy Family went every year to Jerusalem for the feast of Passover. "Every year." But we read nothing else about those many years in Nazareth. Their daily life—days, weeks, months, years—is passed over in silence. Jesus was weaned. He learned to play, to read, to study. He grew tall, became strong. And Mary kept house, gardened, taught Jesus, helped Joseph, met with friends, attended temple, and prayed.

Like Mary, if you are a mother, your summer years are filled with special events: first tooth, first word, first week without diapers, the first letter drawn by chubby fingers, the first dandelion picked and offered with love.

These years may be touched by fear: chicken pox, falls, fractures, illnesses, and other hurts.

There are repetitive tasks, many of them dull, such as weeding, cleaning, mending, and cooking. Mary performed the same chores, cleaning the same rooms, washing the same clothes over and over again. She was like those of us who are trapped in dull jobs, day after day doing the same tasks. No words of Scripture tell us how she felt. Only silence, silence. Is there a message in this absence of words?

FATHER'S HOUSE

"Yes, I have built you a dwelling,
a place for you to live in forever."

1 Kings 8-12

When Jesus was twelve, he went with his parents to Jerusalem on one of their annual pilgrimages. When it was time to go home, he stayed behind at the temple without his parents knowing it (Luke 2:42-43). Mary and Joseph looked for him everywhere for three days. Three days are an eternity when your child is missing. This means at least two nights, nights when terrible deeds may be done. Which emotions plagued Mary during that time? Fear: was he kidnapped? Guilt: how could she have lost him? Rejection: had she displeased Yahweh so that her child had been taken from her? Anger: why had Joseph allowed Jesus to get lost? Sorrow, worry, terror? These emotions are too familiar to all of us.

When our own children reach adolescence they perform actions, sometimes "without [their] parents knowing it." When this happens, Mary's words paraphrase our own:

"Why did you do this to us?" Although Mary knew that Jesus was "son of the most high," she did not fail to scold him for an action that frightened and saddened Joseph and herself. Victims of glib books on parenting, or lacking inner strength, parents too often fail to discipline their children for actions that are unacceptable. Without correction and guidance from parents, children's unacceptable behavior becomes habitual performance. This leads to individuals who may become maladjusted, unhappy, and frequently immoral adults.

When Mary questioned Jesus about staying behind, he replied, "Why were you looking for me?" Sounds familiar, doesn't it? At twelve, Jesus may have already been Bar-Mitzvah'd, a rite that signaled his approaching manhood, his spiritual maturity. The boy-man Jesus was eager to be an adult, take part in a man's world, be about his "Father's affairs." Luke (2:50) tells us, "But they did not understand what he meant" by his response. So much like us! Frequently we misunderstand our children. Like Mary, we worry.

Scripture tells us so little about Mary's mothering. A key indication of how life must have been in Mary's home is gleaned from Luke (2:51): "He...lived under their authority." Although Jesus was eager to begin his Father's work, he returned to Nazareth and waited almost twenty years before commencing his public ministry. Jesus was divine, but his divinity did not diminish his humanity one iota. So at twelve—eager, anxious to start, full of the natural effervescence of youth—Jesus returned with Mary and Joseph to a small village and bided his time.

What can we suppose from such behavior? It is safe to believe that Jesus had been schooled in obedience, that he had learned to value the opinions of his parents, that he was unselfish enough to submit to parental authority. During the return trip to Nazareth with Mary and Joseph, he listened to Joseph's explanations of a son's role, the need for patience awaiting adulthood.

Some parents expect obedience from their children, while others seek only to indulge them. Though customs change and economic stability waxes and wanes, certain basic needs remain constant throughout the ages. Children will always need consistent, patient guidance and discipline in order to develop the strength to cope with the challenges and demands of life. Discipline is seldom easy, but it is always necessary.

One might have expected that after three days of searching Mary would have run to Jesus and tearfully enfolded him, happy to have found him alive and well. But instead there is restraint, the recognition of his part in their sorrow. In order to be consistent with our children, to discipline them appropriately, we must discipline ourselves. We cannot indulge in angry responses nor yield to materialistic desires to heap toys and joys upon our children. Instead we must provide an island of secure serenity in our homes. Amid the sensory overload of a technological society, humankind still needs peace-filled security, a refuge from the many frauds of life. Our homes should provide this haven. But it becomes ever more difficult.

WISDOM

"Watch for her early....you will find her sitting at your gates."

Wisdom 6:14

According to recent information, fifty-two percent of mothers work outside the home, and "contact" time between parents and children has dropped forty percent in the last twenty-five years. What do such data indicate? We should not believe that women have abandoned traditional roles. Only thirteen percent of mothers want to work full time. Economics and the divorce rate dictate otherwise.

The burden of childrearing and homemaking has rested with women, particularly in the Judaeo-Christian culture of the Western world. But within the last century women have had to assume additional burdens presented by technology and education. Technology, born in the Industrial Revolution, has utterly altered our lifestyle. While the vacuum cleaner, microwave, washer/dryer have reduced worktime and labor, the television, VCR, car, computer, and telephone have restricted privacy and introduced a host of problems.

Education, the priceless gift that frees our mental faculties and helps us strive for self-actualization, also vaults us into careers that make additional demands on our time and energy. It is very difficult to juggle the myriad demands of motherhood, wifehood, and career, and still manage to provide an "island of secure serenity" for ourselves and our families. Where is Mary, our role model, in this endeavor?

Luke (2:19,52) told us that she pondered these things in her heart; we must remember that quality of Mary's: to hold something in our heart and ponder it. To ponder something requires deep thought, concentration, reduced distraction. But can we have this without reduced stress? Deep thought, like so much else, is almost impossible when we are overstressed. We are daily bombarded with articles, books, videos, seminars devoted to stress reduction. We are told to run, jog, walk, swim, do more aerobic exercises; we must drink more water, eat more vegetables, eat less fat—all for the improvement of our health. But isn't our spiritual health at least as important as physical conditioning?

Mary, like us, needed time to ponder, to relate to God. Set aside a time each day for "pondering," time for quiet concentration, for sitting silently before God. One period of time out of each day is essential to maintain our spiritual health, ourselves. Devote at least a quarter-hour to your creator and source of life. It can be early in the morning before anyone else is awake, or late at night after the others are in bed. Think of all the tasks you complete each day, all the responsibilities you fulfill, all the energy you expend. Then you will realize your need for this time.

If we fail to provide for our own core-selves, cease to nurture our own special strength, then we will fail to be present to our children, our spouses, our friends and colleagues, or clients. We will cease to be present even to ourselves. Too often, we become "Joe's mom" or "Tom's wife," seeming to lose our own identity. That is when our self-esteem suffers. But if we faithfully set aside this time, giving God and ourselves priority in our lives, we shall discover a source of energy and peace.

In this way the youthful choices of our springtime will continue to influence us. If we were impulsive, short-tempered, self-gratifying, procrastinators—in a word, un-disciplined—we'll have significant problems in ordering the days of our lives. But self-discipline can be learned and it must be practiced diligently and consistently. It is an essential art for parents, for where will our children learn discipline if not from us? They will not learn it from the media, or in the schoolroom, or from friends.

Discipline is an intimate lesson that should be initiated at mother's breast, where the first lessons of love and trust are learned. The developmental task of infancy is to learn to trust. It can be learned only from a self-disciplined parent who does not scream, abuse, abandon, or overindulge the infant. The self-disciplined person is one who has learned to love, first oneself, then God and others. This love provides a safe, nurturing environment and makes a person secure enough to risk imposing discipline upon children. By demonstrating and expecting self-discipline, we are providing for our children the basic tools for survival.

DIVINE DESTINY

"It was rare for Yahweh to speak in those days; visions were uncommon."

1 Samuel 3:1

Media ads bombard us with unrealistic expectations of life, but life is not easy, as everyone knows. Mary's wasn't, nor was Jesus'. Should we expect anything better for ourselves? If we fail to teach this to our children, we shall do them a great disservice. Already far too many of us, oblivious of this reality, waste our lives in a vain search for an impossible dream. Witness the widespread drug abuse and suicide rates.

Furthermore, our children do not belong to us. We are responsible for them, up to a point. But we are mere-

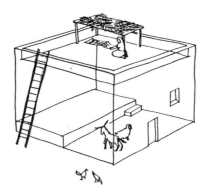

ly their launching pad. God entrusted Jesus to Mary, his mother, and God entrusts our children to us. We cannot begin to know the divine plan for them any more than Mary could know what God wanted of Jesus. We must, however, provide our children with the ability to fulfill their divine vocation.

So as the days slip into weeks, months, and years, we must remember Mary and her home at Nazareth. As Mary did, ponder the events of your own life. Strive to achieve the qualities of her home in Nazareth—not very different from ours: work, weariness, peace, sickness, love, worry, prayerfulness. The silence of Scripture concerning Mary's summer years provides a link for the summer years of our lives.

VESSEL OF HONOR

"Turn again, then, to your God;
hold fast to love and justice."

Hosea 12:7

But what does Mary say to those of us who are not mothers? During our springtime we may have consciously decided to avoid motherhood, wifehood, or both. Or perhaps we are single because of circumstances outside our control. How is Mary our model? In Luke (1:26-38) we read that God sent the angel Gabriel to Mary, who was a virgin. Virginity today is becoming a rare state after age fourteen or fifteen. Lured by some strident proponents of "liberation," girls yield their viriginity, frequently without any shred of commitment.

In Mary's time, casual sex was strongly discouraged, often by the death penalty: the female was stoned to death. Mary's virginity should be seen as an indication that she not only followed a body of religious law and adhered to a code of conduct, but was committed to a way of life in which intercourse had no place outside a committed, caring, married relationship.

We too are highly favored, as Mary was. The Lord is with us, whether married or single. We must believe in the validity of our way of life, the appropriateness of our single state.

In our summer years, it is necessary to live by a code

of ethics. Whether in business, family life, or the professions, the only way to live is as Christians. Like Mary, we must repeat our "yes" to God every day, in big matters and small; we must, to the best of our ability, be full of grace, living in God's presence. We must not, distracted by the demands of everyday concerns, skimp on our commitment to God. When we do, we wonder why we feel lonely, overstressed, burned-out. Too many of us— well educated, well groomed, materially successful—are restless, unfulfilled, floating from one "relationship" to another. We smoke too much, drink too much, struggle through psychotherapy or, conversely, we swim, jog, run, or walk mile after mile to care for our bodies. How much time do we devote to caring for our spirits? We are not grace-filled, highly favored; we have left God behind.

FULLNESS OF GRACE

*"I open my mouth,
panting eagerly for your commandments."*
Psalm 119:131

In her springtime Mary made her commitment to God, and her spirit exulted in God her Savior (Luke 1:47). She never revoked that promise. It is not easy for us to remember or fulfill the promises of our youth, but we have Mary to follow. She who in her springtime uttered the Magnificat, delivered her child in squalor, accepted the homage of the Magi, and fled to exile in Egypt, certainly can provide us with examples of courage, tenacity, patience, sobriety, and purity.

In the fullness of her summer years Mary grew in virtue and, like us, she had no easy time of it. Like her, then, we must seek fullness of grace.

The very silence of the Scriptures enhances our contemplation of her.

ST. JOHN THE BAPTIST
"You shall be called prophet of the most high."

Luke 1:76

Liturgically, springtime opens with the Annunciation, heralding the birth of the Messiah. Summer opens with the feast of St. John the Baptist (June 24), heralding the public ministry of the Messiah. The Masses for John's feast (vigil and Mass of the day) offer particular consolation for women in their summer years.

Frequently in the summer years of our lives we are mired in negative emotions: loneliness, fatigue, frustration. Our spouses are engrossed in their careers; our children, busy with their own lives, still demand our time and attention. Our mirrors reflect the etchings of age; our scales confirm what our clothes have told us.

The vigil Mass reiterates our worth, our unique value to God: "Before you were born I dedicated you" (Jeremiah 1:5). The Responsorial Psalm echoes: "Since my mother's womb, you have been my strength" (Psalm 71).

The Mass of the feastday again reminds us of our worth: "The Lord called me from birth" (Isaiah 49:2) and the Responsorial Psalm proclaims: "I praise you, for I am wonderfully made" (Psalm 139).

Here is confirmation of God's eternal care for us. These thoughts should guide us.

STS. PETER AND PAUL

"What matters is faith,
which makes its power felt through love."
Galatians 5:6

In a few days we encounter the feast of Sts. Peter and Paul. Impulsive, hot-headed Peter, the coward, became a miracle-working martyr, leader of the fledgling church. Paul, the arrogant, proud, Christian-killer became the tireless apostle who endured prison, shipwreck, floggings, and converted many to the Lord Jesus. When we consider the changes wrought in those giants of God through the power of the Holy Spirit, it should cause us to wonder, to be amazed. It should also give us courage to pick ourselves up and continue with God along life's path.

ORDINARY TIME

"Blessed be the Lord, the God of Israel."

Luke 1:68

In the liturgical year the weeks of summer usually fall into Ordinary Time. This is the time following the triumph of Easter, the glory of the Trinity, and the joy of the Body and Blood of Christ: Corpus Christi.

During summer's Ordinary Time the daily liturgies present readings from the "minor" prophets Amos and Hosea (Year 1) or the early books of Scripture (Year 2).

These prophets lead us to the reality of the Messiah: Amos 9:11 and Hosea 2:16-18. The ancient history of Genesis and Exodus brings us beloved family stories. We are all one, and our ordinary days reflect our ages-old pilgrimage toward Yahweh.

Summer's Ordinary Time is peopled with saints: Mary's parents, Ann and Joachim; her contemporaries, Martha and Mary and the apostles; abbots, virgins, martyrs, bishops, doctors of the church, priests, popes, nuns, deacons, widows, parents, and unmarried people.

Their lives cover many courses. Their failures may have been many, but their perseverance, patience, and love for the Lord and others carried them through heroically. And it is safe to assume that each of them loved and esteemed Mary. Many of the virtues that the "summer" saints possessed were present to a greater degree in Mary of Nazareth.

MARIAN FEASTS

*"She is a reflection of the eternal light,
untarnished mirror."*

Wisdom 7:26

Summer boasts several feasts of Mary: July 16, Our Lady of Mount Carmel; August 15, Assumption; August 22, Queenship of Mary; September 8, Nativity of Mary; September 15, Our Lady of Sorrows.

Throughout history humankind has considered certain sites as sacred, special places where God was sought. Mountains in particular have been regarded as holy ground. Croagh Patrick in Ireland was considered a holy mountain long before Patrick fasted and prayed there, prior to converting the Irish to Christianity.

Mount Carmel in Palestine has had a long history as a religious site. More than 800 years before the birth of Christ, it was the site of the worship of Baal. Elijah the prophet converted many people from idolatry by calling on Yahweh to ignite his sacrifice on Mount Carmel (1 Kings 17). Under the title of Our Lady of Mount Carmel, we honor a devotion to Mary that dates back to the thirteenth century. The Carmelites, the order of monks and nuns whose origin is linked to the mountain, have always dedicated themselves to Mary and have given many saints to the service of God.

In the hot steamy days of August we celebrate Mary in

her Assumption and her Queenship. These feasts express our desire to revere Mary's contribution to God's plan of salvation. When we think about the Assumption, we get an inkling of the great love God had for Mary, the extent of God's response to her commitment. Remembering the constancy of divine love should inspire us to develop leadership and influence in the faith-life of our families. Like Mary, we should present Jesus to others, guiding our children toward God. Like her, we should believe that the "promise made...by the Lord would be fulfilled."

On September 8, when we commemorate Mary's birth, the gospel relates the genealogy of Jesus, which is peopled with numerous persons from many walks of life, saints and scoundrels. How fitting that this gospel appears near the end of summer, when the liturgical season presents us with many saints from different backgrounds. Of the seventy-two generations listed as Jesus' ancestors, only four women are mentioned before Mary: Tamar (Genesis 38:1-30), Rahab (Josua 2:1-2), Ruth (Ruth 4), and Bathsheba, "the wife of Uriah" (2 Samuel 11). These women—two widows, a harlot, and an adulteress—what common bond did they share?

Tamar, widowed twice by brothers (Er and Onan), both of whom had deeply offended Yahweh, resorted to duplicity to wrest justice from her father-in-law.

Rahab, a harlot, recognized the God of the Israelites and used trickery to obtain a promise to "save us from death" during the battle for Jericho.

Ruth, a widow, deeply devoted to her mother-in-law, Naomi, married Boaz, an honorable man who took care of Ruth and Naomi.

Bathsheba, seduced by David, married him after her husband, Uriah, was slain in battle because of David's deceit. She became the mother of Solomon.

Their stories have the elements of a modern mini-series: seduction, illegitimacy, political activism, adultery, murder.

They were real women, these ancestors of Mary. Rather than exhibiting fear or lack of ingenuity, they reacted to situations with cunning and bravery. They knew how to adorn themselves with fine clothes, jewels, and perfumes. Living in a male-oriented, restrictive tribal society, they met and overcame challenges, loss of loved ones, danger from war, famine, betrayal. These ancestors of Mary help us speculate about Mary.

Summer's liturgical feasts close with the feast of Our Lady of Sorrows, observed on September 15. As the days begin to shorten and the intense summer heat begins to wane, we are reminded of the enormous price Mary's "yes" cost her.

The entrance antiphon of the day's liturgy echoes Simeon's warning, "Your own soul a sword shall pierce" (Luke 2:34-35). The first reading from the letter to the Hebrews (5:7-9) describes Christ praying with loud cries and tears to God. The gospel reading tells us, "Near the cross of Jesus there stood his mother...." In his last hours, exhausted, dehydrated, bearing intractable pain, Jesus arranged for his mother's care. After his death Mary would have had no one to care for her, but Jesus provided for her. And John, "from that hour took her into his care."

Can we fathom Mary's sorrow? Perhaps in some dimensions. Many women have buried their children, become widowed, have been left homeless. But Mary had been told she was to bear the "son of the most high," whose "reign will have no end." She had "pondered these things in her heart" and had believed that the promise made to her would be fulfilled. How much did Mary understand of Jesus' mission? Scripture tells us she was present at some occasions during his public ministry. In spite of her great faith, did Mary fear that the untimely execution of her son imperiled his goals? In addition to her deep grief, did she perceive the passion and crucifixion as a failure to achieve God's plan? Here again Mary is cloaked in the silence of Scripture. This silence, as we saw earlier, frees us to see Mary through the kaleidoscope of our own experiences. As you have felt your sorrows, Mary has felt hers. Whatever your cross may be, remember, "Near the cross...stood his mother."

The communion antiphon of the feast of Our Lady of Sorrows directs us to "be glad to share in the sufferings of Christ!" As summer slips toward autumn, remember the joy of springtime, the feast of Easter. We frequently enjoy reminiscing about our lives. Reminiscing liturgically is fruitful also.

AUTUMN

*"Does the hawk take flight on your advice
when he spreads his wings to travel south?"*

Job 39:26

During autumn, the season that extends from the fall
equinox to the winter solstice, daylight hours shorten as
the sun slips southward on the horizon. In the northern
latitudes the annual migration to warmer climates begins.
Hummingbirds are restless, anxious to escape the chilling
atmosphere, but the bluejay prepares for the hard winter.
Now in the early morning hours one hears the call of
Canada geese as they leave their habitat. The nights become quiet—no rhythmic cricket sounds, no croaking
frogs. Gardens boast vivid asters and chrysanthemums,
and fruit trees bend under the weight of ripening pears.
Cider and nuts appear in the supermarkets, where the
produce sections are laden with butternut squash and ap-
ples. City folk drive to the country to view the vibrant fol-
iage. Children stand on street corners on a chilly morning, awaiting the school bus. Pumpkins and gourds
decorate porches and entryways. Hardware stores hold
sales of paint, insulation, and other home repair needs.

The autumn mists reflect the general poignancy of
another summer's passing. Nature slows her pace, settling
down, preparing for the dark, cold winter.

WIDOW

"Pity us, Yahweh, take pity on us."

Psalm 123:3

Scripture gives scant information concerning Mary's autumn years. One sad day Joseph died. Was he chronically ill, dying slowly and painfully, or did he succumb quickly, leaving Mary suddenly bereft? We don't know. Tradition paints Joseph peacefully falling asleep in the embrace of Jesus and Mary, both of them present to offer love and solace. But death is rarely peaceful or pleasant. More often it is pain-filled, exhausting, frightening, both for the dying person and for those in attendance.

Mary's sinlessness did not insulate her from normal emotions. Her grief was similar to ours: a heavy heart, a sorrowful mood. Mary knew her beloved Joseph was with Abraham, Isaac, Jacob, but she also realized she would no longer have his comforting presence.

Once again, we realize how like Mary we are. In our autumn years many of us lose our spouses. Some of us suffer shock and anger when they die suddenly; others endure guilty relief after the grinding fatigue of nursing them through long illnesses. Whatever the situation, in our grief and loneliness we can be comforted with the conviction that Mary is real, available to us, and empathetic in our bereavement. She understands the complex emotions of widowhood: loneliness, anger, depression, fear, loss of self-confidence, panic. It's important to realize that these feelings are normal and that Mary, grace-filled, felt some or all of them. Those emotions did not paralyze Mary. She prayed, endured, and continued on with her life.

EMPTY NEST

"Who is there now...to lead me?"

Psalm 108:10

Some time in Mary's autumn years Jesus began his public ministry. Mary's hands, work-worn from years of laundering, gardening, weaving, cooking, and cleaning, were still. Her family life was finished and her home empty, except for herself. When Jesus left for the desert to fast and pray, how did Mary perceive his mission? How had she interpreted the angel's message, the prophecies, the political intrigues, the Roman occupation in relation to her Son? Did she incorporate the canticles of Zechariah and Simeon into her everyday concept of her Son? Was she anxious for his safety? In the evening, after praying, did she stand in her doorway, scanning the road, waiting for Jesus to return?

Or was her luminescent soul already anticipating the Messianic reign?

CANA

"The woman who is wise is the one to praise."

Proverbs 31:30

John (2:1-12) tells us that Mary as well as Jesus was at the wedding feast of Cana. Mary perhaps knew of the invitation Jesus had received and eagerly looked forward to seeing him again.

Weddings are usually cheerful, musical affairs, and Cana was no exception. There were old men chatting with one another about the harvest, women exchanging news as they prepared the food, children running at play, young folk flirting and dancing. Of course, there was also much eating, drinking, and singing.

Mary saw the shortage of wine and was concerned for the feelings of the hosts. Sensitive to hospitality and aware of the nuances of social behavior, she was a take-charge person who saw a problem and set out to solve it. Apparently, she had been in the habit of going to Jesus when she needed his intervention, and although his response in this instance seemed almost curt—"Why turn to me? My hour is not yet come" (John 2:5-6)—he responded to her request by changing water to wine.

How like a mother! In the Temple at Jerusalem she seemed to have held him back from his Father's work. Now at Cana she seemed to be pressing him to begin it. In this single act Jesus demonstrated for all time the importance of Mary; his behavior validates our perception of Mary as our effective intercessor.

Mary issued her directive to the servants—and to all of us forever: "Do whatever he tells you." It was a simple command, yet we have such difficulty with it. We rarely really know what he's telling us. Trapped in busy-ness, fatigue, and illness, or caught up in emotions, plans, and hopes, we fail to hear what he is saying to us. Or hearing, we fail to follow him. We rush willy-nilly through busy days, deaf to Jesus' call. Then when failure, disappointment, or sickness loom, we bewail our fate. Even in our autumn years many of us have not yet learned to listen to him or be sensitive to his presence.

After the wedding feast at Cana, Jesus stayed with Mary for a few days, then returned to his ministry. Luke (4:14-15) tells us that "his reputation spread throughout the countryside." Was she proud of him, as we are when our children are successful? Was there gossip about him when she went to the well for water? Was she afforded any special recognition due to his fame?

REJECTED

"Destined to be a sign that is rejected."

Luke 2:34

One day Jesus came back to Nazareth and "went to the synagogue on the sabbath, as he usually did," where, Luke (4:16-17) tells us, "they handed him the scroll of the prophet Isaiah." Here he was, the son of Joseph the carpenter and Mary. His reputation had preceded him home. What a moment that must have been!

There was silence, with dust motes floating in sunbeams. The people, all filled with anticipation, contempt, hope, doubt—they all listened to him intently. Scripture says the congregation was astonished at his gracious words "and he won the approval of all" (Luke 4:22). But Jesus knew this congregation. He spoke frankly to them, and "was amazed at their lack of faith" (Mark 6:6). They expected marvels to be performed in Nazareth, as if he were some itinerant magician. Jesus knew that even with miracles they would miss the message and not recognize him. His reminder that "no prophet is accepted in his own country" enraged everyone in the synagogue so that they chased him from the place, seeking to kill him.

This was a violent event—men rushing, shoving, yelling, intent on the bodily removal of Jesus to throw him off the cliff. The peacefulness of that sabbath evening was rent by noise. The entire village must have been involved. People either participated in the melee or watched the demonstration without seeking to stop it.

Echoes of that event are heard again in our century: violence, hate, lawlessness.

Where was Mary on that dreadful evening? Was she running along trying to help Jesus? Was she held back as Israelite women so frequently were? In her anguish, did she remember Simeon saying, "He is to be a sign that is rejected"? Luke tells us, "He slipped through the crowd and walked away." Most likely there was no time for explanations or farewells, so Mary was left to face the snide remarks and general disapproval of her neighbors.

How long Mary remained in Nazareth is unknown. There were no compelling reasons for her to remain alone in Nazareth. On the contrary, she would have been most eager to follow him. Tradition suggests that she traveled north to Capernaum to be near Jesus. Luke (8:1-3) notes that there were women who looked after him. Mary may have been part of that group.

NOTORIOUS

"Distressed and starving,
he will wander through the country."

Isaiah 8:21

It is difficult for us to appreciate the impact of Jesus upon his surroundings. The region where he pursued his ministry was largely pastoral, quiet villages dotting the countryside that was given to sheep-raising and fishing. The darkness of nightfall was relieved only by torchlight and moonlight. The nighttime silence was broken only by human voices, the shuffling of cattle, the rattle of a wagon wheel, or the screech of an owl.

There were no televisions, movies, radios, telephones, computers, multiphonic sound, not even a lightbulb! No books, magazines, newspapers to spread news of current happenings. No cars, trucks, planes, guns, bombs, tanks to pollute the land with noise and destruction. The only means of influential communication was through public speaking; aside from letter-carrying messengers, news was generally disseminated by word of mouth.

Just imagine that for one week every television channel, radio station, VCR, newspaper headline, magazine cover carried the same message from one person, and that much of this message was anti-establishment. Then add several miracles witnessed by thousands of people.

Nearly everyone would be shocked, and perhaps frightened. People would discuss this phenomenon. Crowds would gather. Work would slow down. The stock market would react. The person responsible for this would be hounded by thousands of petitioners pleading for help, or conversely, chased by the powerful, seeking to discredit and destroy him or her.

Now take all that emotional reaction and transfer it to Jesus' time and place. Boisterous crowds followed Jesus, climbing hills and fording streams to be near him. They sought his cures, eager for his help. The noisy, emotional multitude surrounded him and allowed him no rest. Luke (5:15-16) states, "His reputation continued to grow, and large crowds would gather to hear him and to have their sickness cured."

This was not an easy time for Jesus. Luke (6:19) tells us that he taught, laid on hands, rebuked some people, saw the faith of others, knew their thoughts, had compassion on them, and "power came out of him that cured them all." Mark (3:20) notes that such a large crowd gathered that they could not even have a meal.

At this point his relatives were convinced that Jesus was out of his mind; they set out to stop him (Mark 3:21). He was working too hard, not eating right, and most of all, he was speaking in a way that would get him into trouble with the authorities.

PRAYER
AND PONDERING

"Now my soul is troubled."

John 12:27

Was Mary somewhere in this situation, rejoicing in his miracles, listening to his parables, concerned about his fatigue, alarmed at the mounting anger of the Pharisees and elders? She was ready to serve him, but was hindered by the multitude of Jesus' followers. So she prayed, pondering all these things in her heart.

Prayer and pondering may sound so submissive, so passive, and women of today frequently reject such a role. In their autumn years they are mature, confident, experienced in the ways of life and very often have reared families. With their children grown and perhaps their husbands deceased, their homes have been empty long enough for them to have overcome loneliness and to enjoy some solitude. Many of them have carved out comfortable niches in their careers. Sometimes they have done both while maintaining long-term monogamous marriages. Most likely, prayer and pondering were not major occupations during their frenetic work-filled years.

And yet, despite their work and successes, many women today are still underpaid in the marketplace, sexually exploited, physically or emotionally abused. Despite the sometimes strident struggles of the feminist movement, many have arrived in their autumn years facing a culture that demeans motherhood and winks at pornography, where divorce, child abuse, crime, drugs, disease, and poverty are rampant. It would appear that society, with all its focus on rights, equality, consumerism, and technology, has failed them.

Many "successful" women interviewed in their autumn years have expressed a sense of loss, of missed experiences, a growing sense of loneliness and isolation. The fulfillment of dreams and the attainment of goals have failed to provide the happiness they expected.

Well educated, well groomed, high earners, professional, they look around and wonder where their years have gone. They express disquietude and a blurred identity. They have been failing in their developmental scale.

In the autumn years of women, prayer and pondering may just be a large part of the answer to their needs. Prayer and pondering will recharge their tired souls, and rekindle their jaded emotions. Prayer is still effective conversation with God. Pondering is a quiet, reflective state of mind, like meditation.

When we see our adult children working too hard (or not working at all!), not eating right, rejecting religion, then, like Mary, we must pray and ponder.

If throughout the previous stages of our lives we have failed to learn how to pray and ponder, we are offered another opportunity to cultivate these essential spiritual skills. Psychology teaches us that developmental tasks not completed during the appropriate years must be re-addressed at a later time to maintain mental health. Just as there are developmental stages and tasks in the physical and psychological spheres, so too in the spiritual realm. Too often we are well read, mature, socially experienced, but spiritually, we are barely literate, stunted, and starved. Unable to sustain a spiritual life, unable even to admit that there is a spiritual life, we fall prey to a host of psychiatric or psychosomatic ills. We suffer from poor self-esteem, melancholy, anxiety, depression, hostility, obesity, ulcers, migraine, addiction, and colitis. We then seek solace in pills and alcohol.

It is time to collect our thoughts, pondering them in our hearts.

FULLNESS OF YEARS

"You will be founded on integrity; remote from
oppression, you will have nothing to fear."

Isaiah 54:14

When we have reached our autumn years, we are running out of time and opportunity to cultivate a healthy spiritual life. Almost the last developmental task identified is integrity versus despair. This task is assigned by Erikson to old age, our winter season.

Millions of dollars and countless hours are spent seeking spiritual solace from TV evangelists, New Age religions, spiritualists, and witchcraft.

It is time to return to Scripture for guidance and solace and to emulate Mary. In our fullness of years, we must be present to Jesus, to our families, and to ourselves in a prayer-filled self-confidence. It is time to develop wisdom, learning it during quiet encounters with God.

ST. MATTHEW

"And he got up and followed him."

Mark 2-14

Like the previous seasons, autumn opens with a "herald-ing" feast. September 21 is the feast of Saint Matthew, apostle and beloved evangelist who listed for us the an-cestors of Jesus, Mary, Joseph. His gospel emphasizes that Jesus is the fulfillment of Hebrew Scriptures. The lit-urgy of the feast stresses our role as Christians: "Go and preach" in the entrance antiphon, and "Live a life worthy of your calling" from the letter of Paul to the Ephesians.

The gospel is taken from Matthew's personal account of his call to follow Jesus. Matthew was a tax collector, a job despised as almost traitorous to his people. Again we witness Jesus calling the outcast, the marginalized. "I did not come to call the virtuous, but sinners" (Matthew 9:9-13).

So, in our autumn years, if we are not as virtuous as we should be, remember that Jesus still calls us and that we must get up and follow him.

ORDINARY TIME

"He safeguards the steps of the faithful."

1 Samuel 2:19

Autumn's liturgical calendar continues with Ordinary Time. The Responsorial Psalms for the 25th week are especially appropriate for the autumn woman: "The Lord has done marvels for us" (Year 1). This reaffirms the fact that God is with us always; our accomplishments, our joys, even our trials have at least been permitted by a loving God. Our failures have made us no less lovable to God. Lest we stumble, another psalm of that week tells us, "Your word, O Lord, is a lamp for my feet" (Year 2). So often we expect to be in control, to make our own decisions. (Sometimes we like to make everyone else's decisions too!) But a lamp to guide us implies going forward one step at a time, because we can't see very far ahead with such a light. It illumines only a few feet of pathway ahead of us. So in autumn if we haven't learned to trust God, to surrender some of our pride, we must, like Mary, believe that the promise made will be fulfilled.

"In every age, O Lord, you have been our refuge" (Psalm 90) from the Mass of the week (Year 2) is yet another source of consolation for us. "In every age" marks our own transition from girlhood to mature womanhood. It also marks the time from "before the mountains were born" (Psalm 90) until eternity.

The readings from the liturgy of the 26th week are taken from Zechariah (Year 1) and Job (Year 2). Zechariah sought to encourage his people after they returned to an impoverished Jerusalem from almost fifty years of exile in Babylon. Job wrestles with the existence of evil. The feelings evoked by these readings may be sombre, not unlike our autumn moods. But the Responsorial Psalms encourage us: "Lord, bend your ear and hear our prayers" (Psalm 17, Year 2), "God is with us" (Psalm 87, Year 1), and "Guide me, Lord, along the everlasting way" (Psalm 139, Year 2).

Throughout this segment of the liturgical year, Luke's gospel leads us to Jesus. He reminds us that "the Son of Man has nowhere to lay his head." Jesus teaches us to pray, and rebukes the Pharisees for their contempuous lack of charity. In Luke (13:10-17) Jesus says: "Woman, you are free of your infirmity." Contemplate these words; make them the theme of your autumn years.

Like summer's, the autumn liturgical season is peopled with saints who were martyrs, priests, apostles, bishops, royalty, angels and archangels, and women who were simple nuns and a doctor of the church.

ALL SAINTS
AND ALL SOULS

"I see him—but not in the present,
I behold him—but not close at hand."

Numbers 24:17

The culmination of saintly feasts is November 1, All Saints Day. On this glorious day the liturgy remembers not only the famous—St. Thérèse, St. Teresa, St. Ann, St. Francis of Assisi, St. Vincent—but also the many saints not identified by name. Our own familial community is present in that multitude: our ancestors, parents, siblings; perhaps our spouses, children, and friends.

All Souls Day, November 2, is assigned three different liturgies. The cry of Job from the first liturgy sums up our destiny: "From my flesh I shall see God." Mary was the life-bearer who brought Jesus to us—in the flesh. This feast reminds us that each of us has a destiny to see God.

Loneliness can be dispelled when we remember the sheer numbers and varieties of peoples who have preceded us along life's path and lived as saints. The readings from Ecclesiastes (25th week of Ordinary Time, Year 2) remind us: "There is an appointed time for everything...for every affair under the heavens." God has not forgotten anyone.

MARIAN FEASTS

"I will instruct you...
I will watch over you..."

Psalm 32:8

Autumn presents three Marian feasts: October 7, Our Lady of the Rosary; November 21, the Presentation of Mary in the Temple; December 8, the Immaculate Conception.

The feast of Our Lady of the Rosary commemorates the times when thanks were offered to God for military victories (first at Lepanto in Greece in 1571 and in Hungary in 1716). The victories were attributed to Our Lady's intercession after many prayers were offered, especially the Rosary.

The reading from the Mass of the day re-presents the Lucan narrative of the Annunciation. Once again, we are reminded of Mary's consent and commitment to our redemption. We must renew our own consent and commitment.

On November 21 we commemorate an ancient tradition given to us by the Eastern church observance. This tradition held that Mary was brought by her parents, Joachim and Ann, to the Temple at Jerusalem and dedicated to the service of God. This occurred when Mary was still a little child, a toddler.

December 8, the Immaculate Conception, occurs during Advent, when we prepare to celebrate Jesus' actual birth and anticipate the arrival of Jesus in our hearts. On this feast we also celebrate Mary's unique privilege: without compromising her free will, God anticipated Jesus' redemptive life by preserving her from original sin. At the moment of her creation, she is redeemed; she is the firstborn of Jesus' Mystical Body.

Mary is the Christ-bearer for all time. At Bethlehem she was the Christ-bearer in the past; through her constant intercession and presence she is Christ-bearer during the present, and she will continue to be Christ-bearer throughout the future.

ADVENT

"Be quiet before Yahweh,
and wait patiently for him."

Psalm 37:7

As the autumn days grow colder, the sun slips farther
south, casting a pale light. As nights lengthen and nature
slips toward winter, our hearts are warmed in anticipation of the feast of Christmas, heralded by the beginning
of Advent.

The readings in the Advent liturgies are dominated by
Isaiah and John the Baptist. Isaiah, written some eight
centuries before the birth of Jesus, describes the Messianic Age. Lyrically beautiful, the themes dovetail with the
other themes from the second readings.

The readings of the Advent Masses present many spiritual ideals for our consideration. The 1st week exhorts
us to wake up (Romans 13:11, Year A) and walk in the
light of the Lord (Isaiah 2:3), while Jesus warns us to stay
awake, since we do not know when the master is coming
(Matthew 24:37-44).

A theme from the 2nd week accents "knowledge" of
Yahweh (Isaiah 11:9) gained from "instruction" (Romans
15:4, Year A), and exhorts us to "make ready the way"
(Mark 1:1, Year B; Luke 3:1, Year C).

Joy, patience, love, and sharing are stressed during
the 3rd Sunday's readings.

Finally, the 4th week's readings are full of faith: "I have been with you" (2 Samuel 7:9), and "Believe and obey" (Romans 16:25-27, Year B).

In Advent liturgies we again encounter the stories of the Annunciation, the Visitation, Mary's own physical advent as she awaited Jesus' coming. As autumn women, we reread these stories with a perspective that is different from our springtime reading of them.

Elizabeth, late in the autumn of her life, bore John, of whom Jesus said, "History has not known a man born of woman greater than John the Baptist" (Matthew 11:11). Scripture is replete with autumn women who brought forth children destined to fulfill God's plan. Here is more comfort. Late in autumn, as we begin to feel superfluous, we are reminded that we still have intrinsic value. As autumn women we must continue to be life-bearers, continue to carry Jesus in ourselves, and to our families and our communities.

The liturgies remind us, in autumn, of Mary's youth and we reminisce about our own youth. Have we kept our commitments? Have we remained faithful to the promises we made then? If our journey toward our autumn has been less than satisfactory, if our sorrows outweighed our joys, Advent gives us yet another opportunity to heal ourselves, to heal our relationships with others, to prepare for another coming of Our Lord. If we have not been faithful to the commitments made earlier in our lives, we can now make a new beginning. In our autumn years, our Advent pondering should focus on all the comings of Jesus: in past time at Bethlehem almost two millennia ago, in future time when our world as we know it will be no more; and in current time, into our daily lives and into our souls, sacramentally. Jesus, Mary's son, enriches our spirits every day, every season of our lives.

WINTER

*"He gives an order...to spread snow
like a blanket."*

Psalm 147:15-16

Winter is the season that extends from the winter solstice to the spring equinox. The northern latitudes, blanketed in snow and ice, lie quiet in the brief daylight. Inclement weather drives everyone indoors, in search of shelter. Those who must go outside do so clad in layers of garments. In the oppressive winter darkness, people seek to dispel the gloom with myriad lights. The piercing wind challenges city commuters. And homeless people die in doorways, unable to withstand the cold.

Vegetable plots and flower beds are desolate, dreary, frozen. The landscape is dull and colorless. There is a sense of foreboding as gaunt oaks creak and groan against the wind. For many animals, activity slows down as they lie in semi-hibernation. Only the hardiest birds—the junco and sparrow—hop about, seeking sustenance.

INTEGRITY

"His faithfulness endures from age to age"

Psalm 100:5

Winter women face a momentous task. They have reached the ultimate stage of human development, which Erikson calls the age of integrity. The dictionary explains "integrity" as the state of soundness, wholeness, or completeness. At this phase of life, then, women must be sound, whole, and complete. In the face of diminishing or altered health, the loss of loved ones, forced retirement, change of residence, a stern realization that one is at last "old," women are expected to become whole, all the pieces finally fitting together. As death draws closer, women in their winter years are expected to become "complete."

Prior development began in infancy when trust and hope were to be developed. Ensuing stages should have taught autonomy, initiative, competence, identity, love, nurturing, and the beginnings of wisdom.

Now the developmental task is to put it all together, to create from the past a new psycho-socio-spiritual whole. How appropriate that the final task is to re-create, to integrate, in a sense to be born!

At last one begins to comprehend the validity of the mystics who compared earthly life to a momentary transition from one eternity to another.

CHALLENGE

"You shall find your tent secure."

Job 5:24

Women in their winters face new challenges. Nearing the biblical "three score and ten," many have outlived their spouses, siblings, friends. Some, like Mary, have buried their children. Living on fixed incomes, they must re-evaluate their living conditions. They may have to move to smaller quarters or share living space with adult children. Possessions lovingly stored in attics or closets for decades must be examined with a critical eye: what to save, what to throw or give away. Beloved furniture and bric-a-brac must be discarded or given away. Sometimes women this age are admitted to "adult communities" or nursing homes. These changes diminish independence and threaten peace of mind.

But women today are not the first in such situations. Consider Mary. Acts (4:32-33) relates that "no one claimed for his own use" anything he or she had. So Mary, living in community, had given everything away. She saved nothing; she had ceded any independence that was hers.

However, there is great peace in recognizing one's utter dependence on God, and not on things. Released from pride and anxiety, the winter woman finally learns, like Mary, to say, "Let it be."

LEGACY

"But I will rejoice in Yahweh.
I will exult in God my savior."

Habakkuk 3:18

While we are in our winter years, our daughters are in their summer years. Many of them are on the mother/ wife/career track. They need our encouragement and example to develop the practice of praying and pondering on a regular basis.

We may have grandchildren to enjoy. Our interactions with them should help diminish some of the isolation of the youth in our present culture. As grandparents, we are free of the many responsibilities of parenthood. Our relationships with our grandchildren are less autocratic, less critical. Through affection, praise, and reminiscence we can bring serenity and joy into their lives. Our peaceful, joyous, and faith-filled attitude is a powerful example for them to absorb.

"Little old ladies," perhaps almost feeble, we can exhibit the core strength developed throughout the seasons of our lives to our daughters and granddaughters.

But what if our lives are such that our adult children or grandchildren are beyond our nurturing influence? What can we do if our loved ones have rejected our faith? They may be hedonistic, or selfish. Or they may be mired in addiction. When did Mary ever have to deal with such problems? What can we learn from her?

Mary was a Jewish woman, a descendant of David. Her blood, her culture, her faith was Jewish. She knew the proud and sorrowful history of her people. She revered Abraham, Isaac, Jacob. She resented the Roman occupation. She studied the prophets and followed the law laid down by Moses and Aaron. From her youth she believed in the covenant between Abraham and Yahweh, and no doubt carefully followed the dietary laws, separating the clean from the unclean. She believed that all males were to be circumcized. She would have performed the ritual washings, and would have withdrawn during her menses. She believed that the Jews were Yahweh's chosen people.

Now the young church, led by Peter and Paul, had decided that the good news must be preached to everyone: Jew, Gentile, pagan (Acts 10:1-35). The rite of circumcision was no longer required (Acts 15:1-10)! Even some dietary laws were relaxed.

How did Mary react to such changes? Perhaps she was stunned and scandalized. She had never heard of Jesus repudiating the very laws, beliefs, and customs that were now being challenged. In all her ponderings she had never anticipated such a development. What kind of morality was developing around her? The infant church seemed to be veering away from all she had believed and loved. How impotent and threatened she must have felt. How difficult for a woman in her winter years to integrate when everything familiar was changing!

THEOTOKOS

"She was pregnant and in labor,
crying aloud in the pangs of childbirth"
Revelation 12:3

After Pentecost marvelous changes occurred. Thousands joined the Christian community. There were cures, expulsions of evil spirits. Peter and John were preaching unceasingly, and later arrested and flogged (Acts 4:1-22; 5: 17-42). Stephen was stoned.

This was not an easy time for Mary. Jesus had entrusted her welfare to John. Would John, like Jesus, be taken from her? Did the violence of the times frighten her? Did she compare these times to the days of Jesus' public ministry?

Although she was full of grace, "highly favored" (Luke 1:29), Mary was no longer young. She wearied more easily. She missed the physical presence of her beloved son and feared for the lives of the apostles. Although revered as the mother of the Lord, Mary had little active participation in the evangelization of the populace. Still bound by the Jewish code of conduct, she would have worked with the women. The heavier tasks such as laundering and carrying well water were no longer expected of her. But Mary baked bread, mended, babysat, prayed, and pondered, still offering her "yes" to her God.

Mary's Pentecost must have been the culmination of

her vocation. All her prayer and pondering had led to that moment, the birth of the church. Now, again, she was reliving the tumultuous years of the growth and development of a body of Christ: the church, his Mystical Body. As she had been an essential instrument in bringing the physical Christ to us, now she was an essential instrument in bringing the mystical Christ to us. She was theotokos: God-bearer.

And she was doing this by baking, sewing, baby-sitting, praying, and pondering.

PRAYER
AND PONDERING II

*"His mother stored up all these things
in her heart."*

Luke 2:52

There are times when praying and pondering seem to be the most difficult actions we can undertake. When we are nearly hysterical with fear for a loved one who seems to be destroying himself physically, mentally, or spiritually, it becomes almost impossible to pray. Our energies are focused on action. We try to intervene in any way we can: physical care, advice, lectures, money, shelter. And all of this is usually to no avail. Sometimes, then, we see the folly of our behavior. Try as we may, we cannot change some situations.

When we finally accept that fact, then we can move ahead. Turn to Scripture. Read Mark 14:32-42. Jesus experienced "sudden fear" and "great distress." He suffered not only on Calvary, but during all the seasons of his life. He said in Gethsemane, "Wait here and keep awake." Mary's life could be paraphrased in just those words. So could winter women's, we who have "seen many days"...we must wait here. We must believe that "not one is lost" (John 17:12). We must pray.

In the face of situations beyond our control, in areas where we are totally powerless, we must emulate Mary and learn from her life, which was fraught with the challenges, the joys, the sorrows, the "everydayness" that we encounter. Turn to Scripture for courage and guidance. Reiterate your "yes" to God.

Studying Mary's life reveals definite consistencies in her behavior. Mary was faithful to her commitments. She was calm in crisis. She traveled when necessary. She was supportive of others. She did what had to be done. Mary prayed, pondered, and believed that the promise made to her would be fulfilled.

SPIRITUALITY

*"I hear my Beloved; see how he comes,
leaping on the mountains,
bounding over the hills."*

Song of Songs 2:8

Failure to integrate ourselves during our winter years leads to despair, which is a result of our inability to accept the pains, disappointments, rejections, and failures of life. It may come from fear of a death that annihilates, a death without any redemption, a death that denies any spirituality.

Where would Mary of Nazareth have been without her strong spirituality? A peasant girl pregnant before marriage, almost rejected by her fiance, she gave birth to her infant in a cold, smelly animal stall. Fleeing to a foreign country in fear for her baby's life, she finally returned to a small village where she was widowed. Then her only son got mixed up with his cousin in questionable challenge of the authorities and was executed, leaving her in the care of another political zealot.

There's not much in that personal history to recommend it. Yet, add the spiritual dimension. Her son is God. Her life's vocation, theotokos (God-bearer), still continues.

You may think there is not much in your life either, but add this spiritual dimension to it. Use this perspective to help you heal your wounds, to empower you to avoid despair and to grasp wisdom.

The Scriptures, ever scarce with stories of Mary, are silent concerning her activities. There is no record of her death, no reference to her assumption. But there is a message there: focus not on death but on life, not on failing health but on strength. In the autumn years we learned of the need to foster a strong spiritual life. We learned the beginnings of wisdom. Now in these final years, wisdom must blossom in us. Our spiritual posture must be like that of John the Baptist: "He must increase; I must decrease" (John 3:30).

CULMINATION

"Snow may come;
she has no fears for her household."

Proverbs 31:21

Aging in a culture that glorifies youth, beauty, health, and physical prowess is discouraging. Our society expresses concern over the "graying" of America. The media address the prohibitive cost this growing segment of the population presents to the national economy. Young adults express resentment that their salaries are tapped to maintain pension funds for the aged.

Winter women who, like Mary's ancestors, survived wars, civil strife, and plague live in a society that devalues them. Contradictory and unflattering models surround them. Television sitcoms, cartoons, and the comics present ludicrous, toothless, brainless specimens of the elderly. The advertising world displays well coiffed, smiling, active elderly women in need of various cures for everything from dirty dentures to incontinence. Gone forever is the image of the old as the wise, patient, revered historian, repository of worthwhile wisdom and lore.

But just as winter provides gloriously crisp days resplendent with crystal-clad trees, so, too, do our winter years have glistening times. Age gives us a better, truer perspective. Looking back over the years, we wonder where the time has gone. Sorrows have been blunted,

87

pains numbed. The events of our seasons have receded to a comfortable quilt that warms us and brings peace.

Our external beauty has faded but our souls still "proclaim the greatness" of the Lord. We are still Christ-bearers. Our vocation does not diminish with time; rather it is drawing toward culmination.

ADVENT
"My heart exults in Yahweh."

1 Samuel 2:1

The liturgical feasts occurring during winter begin and culminate in an advent mode: looking forward to Christmas and anticipating Easter.

In the winter of our years when we are working toward the completion of life, how appropriate it is that we strive forward liturgically.

Winter arrives in the last days of Advent, when it's the darkest season, cold and barren. Liturgically, though, our souls soar with joyful anticipation. Mass for the first day of winter begins with the joyful antiphon, "Soon the Lord God will come...for God is with us" (Isaiah 7:14; 8:10). It continues: "My lover comes" (Song of Songs 2:8), and "Shout for joy" (Zephaniah 3:14).

The gospel story tells again of Mary's haste-filled trip to Elizabeth. In our springtime it was easy to identify with Mary: young, eager, full of life. Now it is easier to identify with Elizabeth. She "scrupulously observed all the commandments" and "kept to herself." Sometimes winter women, wearied by the trials of life, bury themselves in scrupulosity and withdraw from social contacts. This is not a healthy trend.

Study Elizabeth. Even in her old age she was fruitful.

When Mary came to her, bringing Jesus in her womb, Elizabeth was filled with the Holy Spirit and became the first to call Mary the "mother of my Lord" (Luke 1:42).

The liturgy on December 22 urges us, "Lift up your heads!" (Psalm 23:7). The first reading (1 Samuel 24-25) recalls the story of Hannah who, like Elizabeth, bore a son in her later years. Mary's Magnificat is the gospel of the day. These readings remind us of the vital importance of our vocation to be faithful and bear spiritual fruit in our winter years.

CHRISTMAS

*"Blessed be the Lord, the God of Israel,
for he has visited his people."*

Luke 1:68

The Mass for Christmas Eve contains the beautiful canticle of Zechariah (Luke 1:67,79). We are reminded that God has visited us and shines on "those who sit in darkness and in the shadow of death." Like Mary's Magnificat, this canticle reaffirms the covenant with Abraham and recognizes the Messiahship of Jesus, who is to come.

Christmas is assigned three liturgies: the Vigil Mass, Midnight Mass, and the Mass at Dawn. The gospels are Matthew's genealogy and the Lucan nativity narrative. During the long, dark nights of winter we celebrate: "Forever sing the goodness of the Lord; await our blessed hope, for the people who walked in darkness have seen a great light" (Psalm 89; Titus 2:11-14; Isaiah 9:1).

The Christmas season is an emotional time. We remember, relive the Christmases of our past. We place considerable strain on ourselves. Caught up in family traditions and consumerism, we shop, wrap, tie, write, mail, clean, bake, entertain. Music is everywhere: in shops, banks, malls, airports, cars, homes.

But the gospel for Christmas is quiet. All it says is that she gave birth, wrapped him in swaddling clothes, and laid him in a manger—an animal feeding trough! Unlike us, Mary was homeless on Christmas, without even a tent! When Jesus was born, it was as the poorest of the poor.

In the midst of our Christmas festivities it is essential to return to Scripture. Be quiet. Go into the stable and greet your God. Contemplate the reality of Jesus' birth. Transform the excitement of Christmas into the peace and awe of adoration. Like Mary, treasure this time in your heart.

STS. STEPHEN
AND JOHN

"I can see heaven thrown open."

Acts 7:56

The first feast after Christmas is that of Stephen, the first martyr. "Stephen was filled with grace and power and began to work miracles" (Acts 6:8-9). His discourse in Acts 7 is a concise history of the faith of Abraham and Moses, and an indictment of all who fail to believe. He warns us all, "You are always resisting the Holy Spirit."

As with Jesus, false witnesses were set up against him. Like Jesus too, he pleaded for mercy for his executioners as he was stoned to death. Immediately after Christmas, then, we are reminded of the ultimate passion and death of Jesus (Acts 6:13; 7:60).

On December 27, John, the beloved apostle, is remembered. The reading is from John's first letter (1:1-2):

93

"...we have heard, and seen with our own eyes...we have watched and touched with our hands."

We have not been blessed with such an experience. Yet, we have believed. Like Mary, we have believed that the promise made will be fulfilled.

The gospel (John 20:2-8) recounts Mary Magdalene's discovery that Jesus was not in the tomb. It is John's story of his own conversion: "He saw and believed."

So, within three days we have the birth of the Messiah, martyrdom, resurrection. It is a reminder of the glorious covenant "that our joy may be complete" (1 John 1:1-4).

SOLEMNITY OF MARY, MOTHER OF GOD

"Who is my mother?"

Matthew 12:48

The year begins on January 1 with a Marian feast, the Solemnity of Mary, Mother of God. The title of the feast reminds us that Jesus was human and divine. Giving birth to Jesus entitled Mary to be called Mother of God. What does this mean for women in their winter years? The readings of the liturgy tell us, "The Lord bless you and keep you" (Numbers 6:22-47), and "You are no longer a slave" (Galatians 4:4-7).

In our winter years, we must be aware of and tend to the Mystical Body of Christ. We have grown physically and psychologically from the self-absorption of infancy. We have developed into competent, nurturing women. So too, in our spiritual development, we should have matured from self-absorption with our own welfare, our own salvation. We must grow toward a vision that includes all of God's people. That is our spiritual legacy from the motherhood of Mary.

EPIPHANY

"...members of the same body."

Ephesians 3:5-6

The Sundays following the celebration of Mary's motherhood include the feasts of the Epiphany and the Baptism of the Lord. The readings from the liturgies proclaim, "Rise up; our light has come" (Isaiah 60:1-6), "the light of all peoples" (Preface). All of us are co-heirs, members of the same body. Speaking through Isaiah (42:6-7), the Lord says, "I have called you to righteousness, and have grasped you by the hand."

The joy of Christmas permeates these weeks, while the baptism of Jesus anticipates the ministry of the Messiah.

Joy and anticipation are the appropriate spiritual attitudes for the winter woman.

ORDINARY TIME

"Serve Yahweh gladly."

Psalm 100:2

The liturgical calendar again slips into Ordinary Time when we remember many people who served God as Mary did. Ordinary Time always comforts us with the memory of those countless persons who plodded along, praying, working, failing, but rejoicing in the knowledge of God's presence. They displayed Mary's virtues: faithfulness, commitment, humility, joy-filled service of the Lord.

PRESENTATION
OF THE LORD

"...just as you promised...
my eyes have seen the salvation"

Luke 2:30

February 2 celebrates the Presentation of the Lord. Mary and Joseph, faithful to the Law of Moses, brought Jesus, now circumcised, to the Temple to be presented to God. Two people, well on in years, approached the Holy Family. Simeon uttered the fateful words: the child will be a "light to enlighten," and "a sign that is rejected." He told Mary: "A sword will pierce your soul." Anna, "serving God night and day with fasting and prayer," gave thanks to God for Jesus and "spoke of the child to all who looked forward to the deliverance" (Luke 2:25-38). It is very apparent that Scripture demonstrates how aged persons recognize, praise, and serve the Lord. Like Mary, they are Christ-bearers.

LENT

*"And sadness came over him,
and great distress."*

Matthew 26:37

During Lent the days lengthen. Snow melts. Crocus and daffodils emerge into the cool air. Tiny, hardy snowdrops peek through thawing Earth. On Ash Wednesday the prophet Joel warns us, "Return to [God] with your whole heart, with fasting, weeping, mourning." In the readings, Paul reminds us of our vocation: "Be ambassadors for Christ" (2 Corinthians 5:20). Jesus warns us not to "perform religious acts for people to see" (Matthew 6:1-6), and invites us into an intimate, one-on-one relationship with him. The gospels of the 1st week tell us how to achieve this: Jesus teaches us how to pray (Matthew 6:7-15) and to "love your enemies" (Matthew 5:43-48). In the 2nd week of Lent we pray: "Redeem me, Lord; give light to my eyes" (Psalms 25:11-12; 12:4-5), and "Remember the marvels the Lord has done" (Psalm 105:16-17).

Week by week we remember Our Lord and his sacrifice for us. We respond in love: "If today you hear his voice, harden not your hearts" (Psalm 95:1-2). The lenten liturgies follow the public ministry of Jesus, particularly his teaching about prayer, forgiveness, and the motivation for fasting and good works.

The optional Mass for the 5th week of Lent anticipates

the resurrection. Elisha brings a dead child to life (2 Kings 4:18-21), and Jesus calls Lazarus back from death (John 11:1-45). The 5th week also anticipates the crucifixion. The serpent, mounted on a pole, cured all who looked at it (Numbers 21:4-9). Jesus tells us, "When you lift up the Son of Man, you will come to realize that I AM."

The Old Testament image graphically depicts the gravity of sin, the ugliness of evil. The snake hung up on the pole reminds us of the contradiction of the cross. Jesus was hung on a pole, and all who look to him in faith will be "cured." In such debasement, such defeat, we will come to realize that on the cross is salvation. There is no escape. Each one of us must encounter her personal cross to find God. Only Jesus can call us forth, like Lazarus, from death to life with him.

ST. JOSEPH

*"...a virgin betrothed to a man named Joseph,
of the House of David."*

Luke 1:27

The last winter feast is that of "Joseph, the husband of
Mary" (Matthew 1:16). He was a "man of honor" (1:19)
who "did what the angel of the Lord had told him to do"
(1:25); he did "everything the Law of the Lord required"
(Luke 2:39). That is quite a statement: *everything* required.
How many can boast such an accomplishment?

And yet we have not one word of Joseph's to contemplate. There are so many details about him that are
hidden. We don't know his age, his personality, his pol-
itics, his stature, only that he did "everything required."
We do know from Scripture that he was present to Mary
and Jesus. He played a significant part in their lives. He
brought Mary to Bethlehem. He named Jesus, fulfilled the
Covenant of Abraham for him, and presented him at the
Temple. He brought Jesus and Mary into and out of exile.
He took them annually to Jerusalem. He introduced the
boy Jesus to the Law and the prophets. He taught him
how to live as a man. And then he went to wait with the
patriarchs and prophets for the redemption of humankind
to be completed.

Joseph closes the winter liturgical cycle; he leads us
toward the Annunciation and Easter.

CONCLUSION

"You crown the year with your bounty;
abundance flows wherever you pass..."

Psalm 65:11

The liturgical year is like a wheel, always revolving toward God. As in our lives, echoes from one season are heard in another. Many Christians see repetition or redundancy in the re-presentation of the stories of the Scripture throughout the year. But we must learn to listen for the differing perspectives of spirituality available to us in each rereading.

There are various aspects to the events of our lives. The prism of age alters and colors our perceptions. The lessons for one season can apply to another. Just as we can have snow in April or a thaw in January, so can we experience contradictions in the seasons of our lives.

Frequently the winter woman can display the exuberant joy of youth. Like Elizabeth, she can be a spring-filled stream overflowing its banks.

Conversely, the younger woman who suffers in her springtime can feel the emotional chill of winter. The pain of disappointment can be acute and slip into despair.

Young women suffering from terminal diseases are in the winters of their lives. Developmental tasks have been compressed by the urgency of their situations. When one arises each morning painfully aware of the paucity of time, courage develops, wisdom grows, and the soul matures. Time becomes elastic, irrelevant. The present is all there is. Yahweh is omnipresent.

The seasons of our souls, like the seasons of the year, can be unpredictable. But one element is constant: Mary.

Remember Mary: tribeswoman, handmaid, homeless, bride, mother, widow, theotokos.

Remember Mary: faith-filled, determined, committed, astute, courageous, theotokos.

Remember Mary: adolescent, virginal, fruitful, middle-aged, old, theotokos.

So whenever we are confused, doubtful, distressed, disheartened, remember her directive: "Do whatever he tells you."

BIBLIOGRAPHY

Daniel-Rops, Henri. *The Book of Mary.* New York: Hawthorne Books, 1960.

Deen, Edith. *All of the Women of the Bible.* New York: Harper Brothers, 1955.

Devaux, Andre. *Teilhard and Womanhood.* New York: Paulist Press, 1968.

Flannery, Austin, O.P. (ed.). *Vatican Council II: The Conciliar and Post Conciliar Documents,* vol. I. Grand Rapids: Eerdmans, 1992.

Galbiati, E. *The Gospel of Jesus.* Vicenza, Italy: Istituto S. Gaetano, Strada Mora, 1960.

Gordon, Suzanne. *Prisoners of Men's Dreams: Striking Out for a New Feminine Future.* Boston: Little, Brown, 1991.

Jones, Alexander, (ed.). *The Jerusalem Bible.* Garden City, N.Y.: Doubleday, 1966.

McNamara, James. *The Power of Compassion.* Ramsey, N.J.: Paulist Press, 1983.

Peck, M. Scott. *The Road Less Traveled.* New York: Simon & Schuster, 1978.

Stevens, Clifford. *The Blessed Virgin.* Huntington, Ind.: Our Sunday Visitor, 1985.

Stuart, G.E. (ed.). *Peoples and Places of the Past.*

Warner, Marina. *Alone of All Her Sex.* New York: Alfred A. Knopf, 1976.